SECRETS OF A
TOP SEO PRO

Learn Local Search Engine Optimization
While on a Short Flight

BY PD GATES

First Publishing in 2018

Book Layout by Pankaj Runthala

Table of Contents

Introduction

About the author

PD (short for "Powder Dancer") Gates, the only living boy, takes his motorcycle out one afternoon for a ride along an alpine lake. The sun is setting and there's a magical coolness and crispness to the air that is unique to the Rocky Mountains in the fall.

He sees a banner for a music festival. It's free and he has nothing else to do—so he figures, why not? A band takes the stage, one guy and one girl. They start rocking, absolutely crushing it. Their songs are fantastic and he can't believe he has stumbled across one of the best bands and best live performances he has ever seen. Concert over, he hops back on his motorcycle awestruck and rides off to a tremendous firework display that lights up the winding mountain road. He feels like Benny "The Jet" Rodriguez playing baseball on the 4th of July, and as he zips around a curve, laughs like a madman.

(By the way, the band is *Shovels & Rope* and their best song that night was "Birmingham.")

These types of experiences are frequent for me these days. They didn't used to be. I used to be your average stressed and tired businessperson dealing with the pressures and expectations of corporate America.

Who do I have to thank for escaping that life?

Many people, but these especially deserve mention:

1. My parents. They have been 100% invested in me every day of my life. They have both sacrificed a ton for me (well beyond what I would consider to be reasonable) in order for me to have every opportunity to be happy and succeed, and I am very thankful for that.

2. A close friend who brought an enormous amount of strength, faith and energy to this venture that I lacked at the time. This is a truly rare individual who gives greatly to others without a second thought, even when she has nothing to gain.

3. A small group of SEO clients who have been with me since I started my company. I am grateful for their tremendous loyalty, the way they have ignored

hundreds of calls and emails from other SEO companies aggressively soliciting their services, and their patience with my mistakes. All in all, they are really outstanding people to work with. I will always remember the most backward negotiation in business history that happened not long after the company's inception: I quoted a price and the business owner simply said, "I want to be your most important client. I will pay you double that."

PD Gates is not my real name. There's definitely part of me that would like to publish my first book under my real name, and if my SEO company wasn't still active, I definitely would. Out of loyalty to current clients, I am choosing *not* to reveal my name or the name of my company. I don't want people digging into the online presence of my clients with a microscope and figuring out where we obtained their backlinks and things like that. You will see in the following chapters that in order to be really successful at local small business SEO, you have to be willing to bend the rules a bit. No one is going to do you any favors. If you think that a bunch of other webmasters are going to stumble upon and link to that great new blog post you just published, or that every customer who walks through the door is going to write you a flattering review on Google Maps out of the goodness of their heart, you're living in a fantasy world. For the long-term prosperity of my clients, I remain anonymous.

Who This Book Is For

This book is for anyone who wants to execute their own SEO.

It's also for anyone who has ever been screwed by an SEO company and flushed money down the toilet with a campaign that didn't get results or left you in worse shape than you were in before hiring them—meaning you got penalized by Google!

This book will help you do your own SEO, or help you hire a good SEO company if you don't have the time or energy to do it yourself. The key message here? *Get educated.* I can't emphasize enough how important it is for you to be informed before hiring an SEO company. You need to be knowledgeable enough to distinguish truth from BS; you don't have to pass the Bar or get a PHD to call yourself an SEO professional. Any random Joe can start an SEO company.

I have tried to strike a balance between being so overly simplistic that everyone can understand—but the information I provide isn't truly actionable—versus getting so technical and advanced that only someone who has been doing SEO full time for a decade could understand what I am talking about. When introducing a concept that might be unfamiliar for a decent percentage of the readers, I have tried to include a link so you can learn more about it.

This is not a step-by-step guide. It's more of a resource to leverage in order to understand core SEO principles, gather killer techniques that businesses can leverage, and learn to steer clear of the mistakes that I have seen hundreds of others make that have gigantic negative consequences.

I know how busy people are, so I have tried to be as concise as possible. I think that you will be able to read the whole book in one nonstop domestic flight.

Why Reveal the Secrets?

Any time that someone claims to be revealing valuable secrets, it's fair and reasonable to wonder why they would choose to release that information to the public. What does this person have to gain from sharing their knowledge?

It's important not to automatically write off such claims though—people do reveal highly valuable information, and everyone has their own reasons for why they choose to do so. For example, Edward Thorp could have made an absolute fortune if he had hoarded his discovery about how to beat the game of blackjack by counting cards. He didn't have to publish Beat the Dealer, but he did anyway. I won't speculate as to his reasons why, but here are mine:

1. I am at capacity in terms of the clients I can manage and don't have any interest in hiring more account managers or growing the company. I learned fairly early on in my entrepreneurial career that higher revenue does not

necessarily equate to higher profits. Let's say I am feeling ambitious and hire a few more account managers. Then I have to line up a salesperson or two to land enough business to keep the account managers busy. Then I have to spend a bunch of money on advertising to get the salespeople leads. At the end of the day, do I make any more money in that scenario? Maybe…but it's certainly not guaranteed. Right now, I don't spend a dime on advertising or sales, and I'm perfectly content with the size of the company as it is.

2. A wise guest speaker at an entrepreneurial club back in college (I don't remember who, unfortunately) once said something along the lines of, "Everyone is so protective of their ideas for new businesses and thinks that their ideas are so valuable and unique. However, ideas are a dime a dozen. It's really not about the idea; it's about the execution of the idea."

   I have found this to be 100% true. Ideas are a dime a dozen and it really is the execution of the idea that's the challenging part. I can provide a lot of valuable information here, but can one of my competitors take and apply it in a truly efficient and scalable manner? Maybe… but it's not so easy.

3. I really enjoyed writing this book. I don't ever get to do things like this in terms of my daily responsibilities,

and I think my brain was really craving something more creative. Time flew by while I was working on this project.

SEO Gives People What They Need, When They Need It

Those who have or have had really successful SEO campaigns know how incredibly valuable it can be. Successful SEO can be truly transformative for a company. It can turn a break-even venture into a truly profitable marketing machine. Increasing your revenue by a factor of five, or obtaining a through-the-roof-ROI on your online marketing of something like 50 (generate $50 for every dollar you invest in SEO) is really not too rare; most businesses aren't chasing after some miniscule 15% return here.

When you use traditional campaigns like TV commercials, billboards, radio and even Facebook Ads, you're shoving your message down peoples' throats, most of whom have no interest in it. *With SEO, you're giving people exactly what they are looking for at the exact moment they need it.* If someone needs a locksmith in Seattle because they're locked out of their car, the company with 150 five star reviews that shows up at the top of Google's search results for the keyword "Seattle locksmith" is going to get a very, very high percentage of the calls!

This book will focus mostly on local SEO for small businesses, as that's my expertise. The difference between local

SEO vs. national SEO: for local SEO, you are trying to show up in a specific city, whereas for national SEO, you are trying to show up for the entire country.

There's no reason for a small auto repair shop in Reno to show up in Google for a person in Tennessee (in most cases anyway). So the shop would just target "Reno auto repair" keywords. This would be considered local SEO.

On the other hand, a company that manufactures bike racks for vehicles and sells them on their website would want to show up for people across the entire US (or world), and rank for terms like "bike racks for cars," "bike carrier for SUVs," and keywords like that. This would be considered national SEO.

So if you own a small law firm, landscaping company, flower shop or any kind of business that markets to a specific city and want to conduct local SEO, you will find a *ton* of value in this book.

There's still value to be had here for those engaging in national SEO… it's just that the techniques you use, the challenges you face and the priorities of your campaign will be different than that of a small local business.

The Secret Sauce of Local SEO

When it comes to local SEO, there are three main things you want to accomplish:

1. Show up at the top of Google Maps and regular organic results for the keywords that potential customers are using to search for your business

2. Have more reviews on Google Maps than any of your competitors

3. Have a five-star rating

That's the secret sauce. It really is that simple. This book is devoted to helping you accomplish that.

What You Will Learn

Here's an overview of some of the essential topics covered in the following chapters that will put you on the winning side of the SEO game:

- What to do if you get penalized
- How to select a good SEO company
- The items that factor into what I call your "Total Web Presence"
- The danger of bad links and how to repair them
- Why stability and consistency is a big deal
- The importance of and how to obtain online reviews
- What blogging can and can't do for you
- Why you should consider having a YouTube channel

- How social media helps your ranking on Google
- How and when to use paid search
- What not to waste your time on

Whether you are a Do-It-Yourselfer ready to try SEO on your own, or a small business owner who plans on hiring a company, reading this guide will familiarize you with the nuts and bolts so that you end up with a site that puts you out there in front of your customers when they need you.

Let's get started.

CHAPTER 1

How to Spot
the Bad Guys

How can you screen out a bad SEO company that simply tells you what you want to hear if you don't know the industry yourself? It is *extremely* common in the SEO industry to deal with slick salespeople who have never actually optimized and successfully obtained #1 positions for competitive keywords on Google.

Oftentimes, once the contract is signed, you never hear from Mr. Slick Salesperson again and are assigned to an account manager who outsources most of the link building and other work to a company in India. The company in India uses really cheap and automated techniques to build links and within a few months – BAM! – your website is penalized by Google and you're looking at either having to start with a new website from scratch, or pleading with Google via a disavow report to reclaim your innocence.

Why Your SEO Company Might Suck

One of the reasons I decided to write this book is that I hate seeing people flush their money down the toilet, and that's what you're doing when you hire a bad SEO company. Many of my current customers came to me after working with other SEO companies, and I saw firsthand the horrible disasters that took us months to fix.

The truth is that when it comes to competitive keywords, for every one honest and capable company in the SEO industry who is fully capable of getting your site ranked #1, there are ten pretenders out there who can't.

The Ten Reasons Why Your SEO Company Might Suck:

1. The company started off as a web design company, figured out that there's money to be made in SEO, and started calling themselves an SEO company one day. The skills required to be a competent web design company and a competent SEO company are completely different. You can't just read a couple blog posts and a book or two on SEO and claim to be a knowledgeable SEO expert.

2. The company is unable to identify the core factors that will actually make a difference in your rankings, call volume and sales. The information they've gleaned from supposed "authority" sources (blogs/ books/ podcasts) is simply bad or wrong and they have no way of knowing it.

3. The salesperson you talked to (who probably works on commission) sounded knowledgeable, but really just told you whatever you wanted to hear in order to close the deal. For instance, it's common to be told that they can fix a penalized site or other critical issue that may be difficult or impossible to correct. It's also likely that you will never hear again from that great salesperson who sold you the package after the contract is signed.

4. The company doesn't do link building, or lacks the expertise to safely build links without getting your site penalized. (More on why link building matters later.)

5. The company has no track record of success. Until a company has taken many, many different websites in different industries to top rankings and kept them there for a long time, they are not qualified to be doing your SEO. Bottom line: ask questions and get references.

6. The staff is overworked. The account managers are too busy and overwhelmed to proactively identify opportunities that will improve your SEO campaign. Did you know that if you're sleep deprived that your brain is probably

functioning about as well as it would be after pounding four shots of tequila? (https://www.ncbi.nlm.nih.gov/pmc/articles/PMC1739867/pdf/v057p00649.pdf) You don't want a drunk person doing your SEO.

7. The company outsources their work to India (or some other country). You would be amazed at how many SEO companies outsource everything to some dirt-cheap overseas company and strictly serve as the middleman. Most of the SEO work that I have seen come out of India has been very poor (there are some really great programmers over there though!).

8. The account managers lack motivation. They likely aren't getting a pay cut or getting fired if they lose a client. Conversely, they likely aren't getting sufficiently rewarded for maintaining a super high customer retention rate and consistently delivering outstanding results.

9. The company is not honest. Some companies have no integrity and have no qualms about covering up their mistakes. You need to do your best to test out their claims for yourself. Google their customers' sites. Dig into their online reviews. Occasional mistakes are inevitable, but you want to hire someone who will own up to their mistakes and do everything within their power to make it right, even if it costs them money. Never entrust your SEO to someone who isn't honest 100% of the time.

10. The company wants to lock you into a long-term contract. When a company claims they need a year to get results, beware. It may be their way of ensuring they get paid regardless of the results they deliver. If your site is brand new and you're going after some crazy competitive keywords, then yeah, it could take a year or a lot longer. However, most of the time when it comes to local SEO, it's possible to get results—higher rankings and more leads, calls and sales—in a couple months or even weeks.

Now that you've been forewarned of some things to watch out for, the rest of the book will be devoted to helping you understand what you need to do to maximize your *Total Web Presence* and get your phone ringing off the hook.

CHAPTER 2

Your Total
Web Presence

Far too many SEO companies are one-trick ponies and just *obsess* over one or two things. They might be super anal about onsite SEO, schema markup, or the way the code is presented. They might repeat "content is king, content is king" like a broken record. They might obsess over link building and spend all of their time figuring out how to land a prominent link on some high authority site.

If you focus more on your *Total Web Presence* (definition coming later this chapter), you will avoid a lot of these common pitfalls.

Consistency and Stability

When discussing SEO topics in the following chapters, take care to prioritize consistency and stability.

Consistency sends a message to Google that you are serious and reliable. Whatever you do, do it with regularity. Daily, once a week, once a month. Whether you're posting on your blog, engaging in social media or posting a YouTube video, work a schedule.

The other factor is stability. Google desires stability, another item that many people botch with their SEO. When it comes to appeasing Google, stability is your friend and volatility your enemy.

Optimally, you'll set up your homepage title tag (https://moz.com/learn/seo/title-tag) right the first time and never touch it again. The homepage title tag is just such a gigantic signal to Google; you want to send a consistent message about what *exactly* your website is all about. Let's say you run an ecommerce website and frequently change the products that you want to emphasize most. If you regularly change the homepage title tag to reflect that, you're doing damage to your SEO. Or, if you're an HVAC company, you wouldn't want to change your homepage title to emphasize "AC repair" in the summer and "heater repair" in the winter. This is a common mistake that beginners make.

If you change your office location every year because the price of the lease increases, or you want to focus on a different geographic area, that's bad for SEO. Likewise, if you change your company name, URL, services that you offer and things like that too frequently, that's bad for SEO. If the links that are pointed at your website keep changing, that's bad for SEO.

Stability is your friend and volatility your enemy.

There's a myth out there that SEO changes all the time and that what's true today likely won't be true tomorrow. There might be a small amount of truth to that (Google does tweak the algorithm frequently); however, there's a lot more stability to SEO than most people think. Google doesn't really just turn everything completely upside down on a whim. And you don't need to understand every single facet of Google's algorithm, or be some programming genius, to obtain top rankings. At a high level, what you're trying to accomplish when it comes to local SEO looks something like this:

> A website that is moderately well-optimized in terms of onsite SEO (https://moz.com/learn/seo/on-site-seo), has lots of other trusted websites linking to it, blogs regularly, gets new reviews on a regular basis (not just on Google but on other sites like Facebook, Yelp and other industry sites too), publishes YouTube videos that

get lots of views and interaction, is active on social media and has lots of likes/followers, blasts their website with PPC, has high traffic and is BBB accredited with an A+ rating.

I would consider this website to have a strong Total Web Presence and it would be *highly likely to rank high in the search results.*

I know. It sounds like a lot. *But we're going to break it down and focus on how to accomplish all of these things individually in a very practical manner.*

Introduction to Total Web Presence - How to Make Your Website Important

Over time, Google's algorithm has shifted from more of a PageRank-based algorithm (https://en.wikipedia.org/wiki/PageRank) to one that considers many different factors.

If that sentence doesn't make much sense to you, that's fine: just know that links pointed to your website from other websites used to be pretty much the only metric Google used to measure if a website is important, but now many different things are considered.

The basic goal of Google's algorithm is to figure out (1) how important your website really is (and therefore how deserving it is to be ranked at the top of the search results) and (2) how relevant a website is to a user who types in a particular keyword phrase.

Think of your Total Web Presence in terms of all of the factors that Google could consider in terms of figuring out how important your website really is. These items include, but are not limited to:

- Number and source of the links pointed at the website

- Quantity, location and consistency of citations (read https://moz.com/learn/seo/local-citations if you don't know what that means)

- Quantity and location of online reviews

- Traffic (unique visitors, page views)

- Social media presence (number of Twitter followers, Facebook likes, etc.)

- Average amount of time the average user spends on the site

- Average number of pages the average user views before leaving the site

- Click through rate (in organic and possibly even in paid search, but I have no proof of that)

- How frequently the website is updated and new content is added

21

- Quantity of original blog posts and the frequency that new posts are added

- Possibly sales and conversions (Google has access to this data if you enable conversion tracking in Google Analytics or Adwords)

Manipulating each of these variables in your favor is the key to successful SEO.

In the following chapters, I'll break these down. You'll find tricks and techniques to increase your Total Web Presence, and you will rank higher in Google as a result.

CHAPTER 3

Onsite SEO Basics

You'll hear people talk about two types of SEO: offsite and onsite. You need to pay attention to both, but many more people go wrong when it comes to offsite.

Onsite SEO - This refers to setting up your website code in a way that Google can easily comprehend what it's all about (and therefore what keywords you should rank for).

You accomplish this with title tags, meta descriptions, page content, header tags, URL structure and a few other ways.

Offsite SEO - This refers to things that aren't happening directly on your website, but are used by Google to figure out how important the site is. Examples would be links from other websites that are pointed at your website and social media presence.

There are many people who can adequately optimize a website in terms of pure onsite SEO, so I am not going to focus too much on it. There are many books out there that devote way too much time and attention to onsite SEO. You can refer to the Google SEO guide and it will give a perfectly fine overview if you want to dig into it more: https://support.google.com/webmasters/answer/7451184?hl=en.

I am sure that there are hundreds of people on freelancer websites like Upwork who could be hired for a very affordable rate who would do a good job with your onsite SEO.

It's the offsite SEO that everyone screws up, so that's what we're going to focus on for most of this book. But first, a few thoughts on onsite SEO:

You Don't Have to Be Perfect When It Comes to Onsite SEO

Most small businesses engaging in local SEO don't really need to get overly anal with onsite SEO. You only need the basics in place in terms of optimized title tags, meta descriptions and text content on key pages that you're trying to get ranked. A search engine-friendly URL structure, optimized header tags and things like that help a lot, but you would be amazed at what you can accomplish even when everything isn't perfect with regard to onsite SEO, if you nail your Total Web Presence.

We have gotten plenty of Wix and Vista Print websites ranked #1, and if it's possible to accomplish a #1 ranking with Wix or Vista Print, I am pretty sure you can accomplish it with any platform.

Wix claims that *"Managing your site's SEO is the most important thing you can do to promote your website online. Short of creating the stunning website itself. Like a digital calling card, good SEO can shoot your business to the top of Google pages and earn you a steady stream of organic traffic."* However, you'll find that the very most basic options that you would want in terms of onsite SEO (things as simple as adding a unique title tag on an inner page!) aren't available with a platform like Wix. Nonetheless, it's still possible to obtain top rankings with a Wix site.

That being said, just because you can get a site to rank high on these awful platforms, it's still far from optimal. If you're starting from scratch, go with Wordpress or just build a responsive (https://en.wikipedia.org/wiki/Responsive_web_design) site in plain HTML. Building in HTML is an underrated option for a lot of small businesses. Wordpress is all the rage, yet it can be frustrating to deal with endless Wordpress/plugin updates. If you don't keep up with the updates, your website is vulnerable to being hacked (which completely screws up your SEO).

One quick trick with regard to your onsite SEO that I will mention: many onsite SEO experts write super boring meta descriptions. If click through rate is a factor in the algorithm, why not write a meta description that will actually encourage people to click on your listing? What will grab their attention? If searchers are skipping over websites that are ranked higher than you are to click on your listing, then you're going to start ranking higher in the search results.

See if you can think of some creative ways to accomplish this.

What are my keywords?

Keywords are the words or phrases that you want to show up for in the search engines. These words should be prominent and repeated throughout your site.

Oftentimes, keyword selection is obvious and straightforward. Let's say you own a moving company in Oklahoma City: some of your primary keywords are going to be terms like "Oklahoma City moving company," "OKC movers," and similar variations.

Include your keywords in the URL, title tags, headers, links, page content and images.

Pitfalls to Avoid

The elementary mistakes that I see some SEO companies make are truly mind-boggling. You would think that if you are going to spend all of this time and money optimizing for a particular keyword, that you would make sure people are actually—you know—typing that term into Google.

Sure, if you're an AC repair company in Atlanta, you can feel good about high search volume for certain phrases without doing any research, but for many obscure products and services, that's not a given.

Here are a couple tools to check how many searches a keyword receives:

1. **Use the Google keyword planner.**

   Go to the "Keyword Planner" tool in Google Adwords. Check out the search volume tool and make sure to use exact match, or else you will get an inaccurate number (enter the keyword as "[ac repair Atlanta]" instead of just "ac repair atlanta"). Also, try the "search for new keywords" option to generate new ideas—this can be really helpful. For a recent client, a synthetic turf manufacturer, I entered the keyword "artificial turf." When I used this tool to do further research, I discovered that the term "fake grass" had high search volume and low competition.

   The search volume estimates here can be helpful, but I haven't found them to be incredibly accurate. You can get a much more accurate idea of volume by actually running some paid search yourself.

27

2. Run Google AdWords.

Run Google Adwords with some exact match terms you are considering, broad modified and pure broad match keywords. Be sure to set a low bid on pure broad match terms; they're unlikely to convert well unless you include tons of negative keywords. Then, after running for a couple weeks and obtaining some data, pull a search query report by going to "Keywords," and then "Search Terms."

I would recommend sorting by impressions from highest to lowest. Here, you can see exactly how many people searched for each keyword phrase. This is your single best source for accurate search volume data. Keep in mind that search volume can be highly seasonal. "Lawn care" terms, for example, are going to get a lot more searches in the summertime than wintertime.

The most annoying part of these search query reports is that sometimes Google will lump a huge amount of data into the "Other search terms" section, which provides you absolutely nothing in terms of insightful data. Seriously, what's up with that, Google?

Learn more about **Paid Search** in Chapter 10.

CHAPTER 4

Location, Location, Location

Here are some huge mistakes that for some reason, people always screw up:

The Location of Your Office

It's really crazy because *this is such a simple one,* but I see it all the time. The actual address of your office has to be in the main city that you want to target. It's a gigantic signal in Google's algorithm for local SEO. Let's say that you own a roofing company in Golden, Colorado that serves the entire Denver area. You really want your website to rank for Denver keywords because there's high search volume there. You might throw this down as your meta data:

- Title Tag: Roofing Company Denver CO | Expert Roofer | "Company Name"

- Meta Description: Serving residents of Denver, Colorado for over 50 years. A+ BBB. Free estimates.

- H1: Call Our Denver Roofing Company Today At XXX-XXX-XXXX.

- Repeat "roofing company," "roofer," "roofing contractor," and "Denver" many times in the paragraphs of content in the homepage/inner pages.

Google is not going to rank you highly and you're not going to show up in Maps for these "Denver" keywords. Roofing companies that are actually located in Denver and have a maps listing with a Denver address have a massive advantage that you can't overcome. Trying to rank for Denver terms is going to be like pushing into a brick wall.

Have a Real Office

This is a big one. Nailing the Google Maps profile is one of the very most important things when it comes to local SEO. People are always trying to save money and take every shortcut you can possibly imagine. Here's the optimal setup for local SEO:

- A permanent presence in the same location for a long time

- A sign in the front of the building with your company name on it, or at least a sign on an office door or in the lobby

- Lots of photos of the interior and exterior posted on Google Maps

- Your business receives mail there

- Leased office space instead of a house/apartment

- A displayed address on your Google Maps listing. If you check the box that says, "I deliver goods and services to my customers at their location," then make sure you check this box as well: "I also serve customers at my business address." (Your address will be hidden from the public if this box isn't checked.)

The further you get away from this optimal setup, the harder it's going to be. PO boxes don't work. Virtual offices *can* work if you really know what you're doing and know how to sneak it past Google, but it's far from optimal. If you get a map listing confirmed at your house and choose to hide the address, good luck ranking for any keywords that are competitive. You're setting yourself up for failure.

SEO companies should set their clients up for success beforehand and either turn down clients that aren't in a position to rank high—in terms of having a real office in the city they want to rank for—or be really proactive before a contract is ever signed by helping them line something up that will work. It's incredibly rare for an SEO company to do that though. Usually, you're dealing with a commission salesperson who just wants to get a contract signed and get out.

CHAPTER 5

Blogging

Blogging can be helpful in terms of local SEO, and it contributes to your Total Web Presence. If you have lots of really interesting, 100%-unique posts that generate traffic for you, that's great. Blogging is, however, **overrated.** It's not really a foundational piece of a local SEO strategy; it's just another tool to leverage in order to increase your Total Web Presence. SEO companies that pitch it as a key component of local SEO strategy probably don't know their stuff. A post every day (even every week) would be overdoing it for many small businesses. Those resources are better spent elsewhere. As mentioned in the "How to Measure Progress" chapter at the end of the book, the traffic that your blog posts generate is unlikely to result in sales.

To sum it up: throw up a good blog post that will resonate with your website visitors every once in a while, but don't obsess about it too much. Emphasize quality over quantity.

Blogging Tips

When you crank out a blog post, make sure to blast out the link on all of your social media platforms. The traffic increase helps your SEO. If you're a pretty good scribe and decide to take a stab at your own blog, here are some basic guidelines to follow:

Make it useful.

Provide information or tips that your potential customer can actually use. For example, if you're in the AC repair business, a good post would be about how often someone should service their unit to keep it running optimally.

Optimize the posts.

Blogging can also increase your site-wide keyword repetition and density. For example, if you're an immigration lawyer, it's a good idea to try to work in a few instances of "immigration attorney" per post. Include links in the post to key landing pages and resources on your website as well. It's not just external links that help your website rank; internal links count too.

Want to blog but don't have time?

If as a small business owner, you don't want to take the time to write blog posts, there are hundreds of content writers out there who will eagerly write 500 words for $10 to $20. For businesses that require specific expertise, such as a law firm that specializes in immigration, either the writer will have to write in a very generic manner, or you'll have no choice but to crank out blog posts yourself.

To sum things up:

Throw up some really solid content that will resonate with your website visitors every once in a while, but don't obsess about it too much like many SEO companies do. You're better off obsessing over other components that contribute to your Total Web Presence.

CHAPTER 6

Link Building

Link building is critical for most SEO campaigns because—to really simplify it—links count as votes and the more votes you have, the higher you rank. Let's face it: people don't just give a great link to a tiny little pest control company or criminal attorney out of the goodness of their hearts. You have to be proactive and seek out opportunities.

I hope that my friends in India will read this chapter because even though I have found them to be hard-working and good people, a high percentage of the really awful link building efforts that harm websites seems to come out of that country. A completely new approach is necessary.

Avoiding Google Penalties

People have done more harm to their websites with irresponsible link building efforts than with all other SEO techniques combined.

Roughly 50% of the potential clients that come to us after working with another SEO company have some kind of issue with bad links, sometimes in the form of penalization. More frequently, they just have really poor spammy links pointed at their website, or had spammy links at one time in the past. Both are bad for SEO. Remember how important stability is? Having a bunch of links pointed at your website—that are then all removed at once because it's learned that they're low value and spammy—is bad, bad, bad.

I have found the website http://backlinkwatch.com to be a decent source of data for links that were pointed at a website sometime in the past. Sites like Open Site Explorer (https://moz.com/researchtools/ose/) only show you current links.

How do you know if Google has penalized your site?

Let's say you're ranking at the top of Google one day, and the next day you're on page 9: it's highly likely that you got penalized. This type of situation became common when Google started pushing out their Penguin updates (https://en.wikipedia.org/wiki/Google_Penguin).

Another good way to figure out if your site received a penalty is to sign up for Google Webmaster. You will get a message about unnatural links.

I want to point out again that although it's rare in 2018 for us to come across a truly penalized website, we do come across sites that are being hurt by having—or having had in the past—spammy crap pointed at them. Hundreds of links from low-quality sites that all have the same anchor text is really bad for your overall link profile. When I pull a website's backlinks and see something like "Detroit electrician" as the anchor text for 95% of its total links, I know I have my work cut out for me.

Here are rules to follow to avoid bad link building and keep from getting penalized by Google:

Rules to Avoid Bad Links

1. Never build a link on a website that exists solely for the sake of selling links. For example, it used to be common for people to create a website all about DWI and load it up with a bunch of DWI-related content. Website relevance would obviously be super high for a DWI attorney, and a quick check on Moz showed decent site authority, so this was a quick, easy and cheap link for a lot of people. Don't do it! Websites that exist for the sole purpose of selling links often get deindexed by Google (meaning Google removes the website that sold links from their

search results). Links that point to your website from a deindexed site are bad news.

2. Don't go for anything cheap or automated. Even though I'm writing this book in 2018, and the *Penguin update came out way back in 2012,* these types of cheap awful link building programs are still all over the place. A quick search on Fiverr reveals the following gigs:

   "I Will Do 5000 Safe Powerful SEO Link Building" – ($5)

   "I Will SEO Link Building Create Da70 High PR Dofollow Backlinks" ($5)

   "I Will Provide 100 High-Quality White Hat SEO Manual Link Building" ($5)

   I still see banner ads for things like "DA40+ PA40+ Backlinks for $6 per Month."

   This stuff is absolute rat poison for your SEO campaign— almost as bad as a member of the media is for an Alabama football player.

3. Avoid any type of service in which you get an article posted all over the web (except for a press release), spinning service and other things like that.

4. Don't join any link trading networks in which you pay some kind of fee to swap links with other websites or

any similar structure. I don't care how slick-talking the owner or salesperson is... run for the hills.

5. Don't worry too much about the "nofollow" tag, which *supposedly* tells Google (via the HTML code) not to follow a link and not to count the link as a vote. If it's a good placement on a high-quality website, accept it with no reservations, even if "nofollow" will be applied. Our company has done studies and found that Google does indeed follow the link and attributes value to it.

6. Don't obsess about anchor text. Just make the anchor text and link look like it belongs on the page. Don't make it look like some SEO guy forced it on the page in an effort to rank in Google. If you approach your link building with something like: I am going to build five links with the anchor text "Indian food NYC," four links with "New York Indian restaurant," and three links with "best Indian food New York," you're doing it all wrong.

How to Build Good Links

Now that you know what to avoid, how and where does one build links?

People tend to get obsessed and crazy about link building, sometimes spending 14 hours trying to land some obscure .edu link without acknowledging the basics. *When it comes to link building, first nail all of the basics before you venture off into anything too ambitious*:

1. Sign up for all the prominent directories in your industry. For example, if you're a counselor, make sure to sign up for all of the major directories like Theravive, Network Therapy, HealthGrades, alltherapist.com, etc.

2. Create a profile on all the high-quality major directories like Yelp, Angie's List, Thumbtack, YP.com, CitySearch, etc. Don't waste time with the really awful low-quality directories that receive no traffic.

3. Create a YouTube channel and upload some videos. Link to your website from the video descriptions and channel homepage. If you don't want to create your own videos, there are plenty of people on freelancer sites like Upwork who will produce really professional looking videos for a very reasonable fee.

4. Sign up for a BBB listing. This is one of the most important citations that a business can obtain because it helps your Maps listing pop. https://www.bbb.org/

5. Have a social media presence on sites like Facebook and Twitter, and link them back to your site.

6. Go after all the really easy links that you can think of. Maybe your web design company is willing to link to you from their portfolio. Maybe if you write a testimonial for

one of your vendors, they will link to your website from their testimonials page.

7. You can shoot out a premium press release here: http:// service.prweb.com/pricing/?nav_location=main_menu. It's not a great source of valuable links and shouldn't be a primary tactic you use but I am sure that there's still some value to be had.

If you nail the rest of your Total Web Presence, that might be all you need to do in terms of link building to obtain a #1 ranking.

Methods to Get More High-Quality Links

Depending on the competition, the items above might not be enough to get you ranked high in Google. Some industries are very competitive and you may need more links.

Here are some other effective methods:

1. **Join or create a tight network of other small business owners.**

   This wouldn't necessarily be a Business Network International (BNI)-type group in which you're pressured to utilize each other's services and things like that, but rather a collaborative and communicative effort in which you can bounce questions off of each other and do small favors for each other. As an example, there would be huge value in a group of lawyers agreeing to include small sections on their websites for referrals:

We routinely receive inquiries for non-personal injury types of cases. We don't personally work in other fields, but feel comfortable recommending these companies:

For criminal law – Firm X

For bankruptcy law – Firm Y

For a family/divorce lawyer – Firm Z

Make sure to include an address and phone number for each firm so they get a citation out of it. There's nothing wrong with a few reciprocal links. Most of your links should be "one way links" though (i.e. the other website links to you, but you don't link back to them from your site).

2. **Place banner ads.**

   Place banner ads (or text links) on forums, online newspapers, online magazines, high-quality and high-traffic blogs and other websites that are trying to monetize their traffic by selling ads. When doing this, you're generally looking for a static banner (i.e. it doesn't rotate with other banners) that links directly to your website (i.e. not some kind of forwarding or affiliate-type link that tracks clicks).

Make sure to negotiate a direct link beforehand. Scroll your mouse over other banners on the website and see if some crazy long forwarding URL displays at the bottom of your browser, or if the actual website URL displays.

You don't get any credit for a forwarding/tracking URL; the link must point directly at your website.

A lot of local newspapers are struggling financially and have started publishing their content online, so they will be happy to take your money for a banner ad or text link.

3. **Sponsorships.**

   A lot of local charities will have a sponsor page, or might even display your logo and website link from their homepage. Look for charities that are based out of the same city that your business is located in.

4. **Article posting.**

   There are some people who will post an article with a link on really high-quality websites like Forbes, Entrepreneur. com, Huffington Post, etc. This is clearly a paid link (against Google's link building policy), but as of right now it's a pretty safe and effective strategy. Focus only on high-quality name brand websites for this and realize it's likely to be expensive. Make sure you're not getting a link on some random subdomain that has no page authority whatsoever. For example, you generally want your article posted on *forbes.com/your-article,* instead of *some-random-*

subdomain.forbes.com/your-article. I mention this because a lot of sites have an option to sign up and contribute as a blogger, and that subdomain is unlikely to carry much weight.

5. **Develop relationships with other webmasters.**

It can be hard work to develop these relationships, but once obtained, they are extremely valuable. You want to reach whoever owns or manages websites that have decent traffic, with topics similar to the websites you are trying to get ranked. So if you want to build links for a family doctor, a website about health and nutrition tips would be a good fit. You want to connect with people who are concerned about maintaining a high-quality website and aren't willing to trash it with a bunch of spammy, unrelated links for a few extra bucks. Like I mentioned above, make sure that the website doesn't exist solely for the purpose of selling links. Ideally, you would be the only person placing links on that website.

One way to develop these relationships is to crawl through Google's search results to find websites that would be a good fit. Then, contact the webmaster and explain what you're wanting to do and see if you can strike a deal. A lot of the time you're not going to get a response, and when you do get a response, you still may not be able to make a deal (they are wanting too much money or are unwilling to post the link in a way that makes sense). Once you do find a good fit though, it's a great connection to have.

This practice violates Google's link building policy, so it's up to you to in terms of how much risk you want to assume.

Best Practices to Follow

Hopefully, these methods will at least get the ball rolling for you. Just make sure when building links that you're:

- Building links on pages that Google actually knows about. Sometimes a page looks great at first glance but Google hasn't even indexed it. Simply go to Google and type in "info:the page URL" to quickly check. For example: info:yahoo.com.

- Manually building high-quality links on high-quality websites and not relying on anything spammy, automated or low quality.

CHAPTER 7

The Underrated Importance of Review Building

If most small business owners and SEO companies obsess too much about blogging and link building, they certainly don't obsess enough about **review building**. I really don't understand why: it's just so ridiculously obvious that a company which consistently appears in Google Maps results and has the most five-star reviews is going to get a crazy disproportionate amount of the calls. Think about it: who are you going to call—the the plumber who has 130 five-star reviews, or the guy who has three reviews and a 2.5-star rating?

Your goal, quite obviously, is to have more reviews than any of your competitors in Google Maps, have a five-star rating, and to get your Maps listing to consistently pop up in the search results.

Review building has other critical benefits you might not have even considered:

1. The Impact of Reviews on Consumer Behavior

Reviews have a psychological impact on the consumer. Imagine you're planning on spending money on an expensive ski-in/ski-out Airbnb vacation rental in Vail. If the property has 75 five-star reviews and none that are negative, how much more likely are you to overlook a minor offense that may occur during your stay and not trash them with a negative review?

It's only natural to assume the offense was out of the ordinary, or maybe even that you're being a bit high-maintenance and need to lighten up a bit. On the other hand, if the property has 50 reviews and a two-star rating, you're more likely to look for something wrong and seek out some kind of retribution, like leaving a negative review or requesting a refund.

2. Reviews Help You Rank

Having lots of reviews helps you show up on Google's first page, especially if you've also taken the time to build reviews on websites like Yelp, Facebook, InsiderPages,

Manta, HomeAdvisor and other sites that are relevant for your industry.

3. Make Life Easier on Your Salespeople

Review building makes the sales process easier. The salesperson who answers the phone will have a much easier time selling your product or service if you've nailed your review building. The potential customer who has seen hundreds of five-star reviews prior to placing the call is much more likely to convert.

Review building can also be leveraged in paid search. The star rating can be pulled directly into the Adwords ad via a location extension (https://support.google.com/adwords/answer/2404182?hl=en). This will increase your click through rate, which increases your quality score, which gets you more clicks for less money. It increases your conversion rate too so that your ROI is significantly higher.

It's a really great idea to build a ton of reviews on TrustPilot, simply for the sake of pulling a star rating into paid search ads.

How to Build Good Reviews

How does one build reviews? You have to ask! Unless you're in the restaurant business and can rely on a horde of wannabe food critics to post reviews for you, you're going to have to reach out and possibly even incentivize your clients to leave a review. Think about it: when's the last time you got an oil change and just left the company a nice five-star review on Google Maps to thank them for their service? Probably never, even though that review would be highly valuable for your friend in the oil change business.

Some review sites—notably Yelp—are radically opposed to you asking for or providing any kind of incentive to your customers for leaving a review. Others review sites really don't care; they just want the content and engagement. If you somehow get caught rewarding a customer for leaving a review for you on a site like Yelp, there could be consequences, including reviews being removed from the profile or even some kind of profile suspension. I have never experienced this but have read about it happening.

When asking or incentivizing your customers to leave a review, consider something like a $10 gift card or a discount on your services. Some things to keep in mind when crafting your review building strategy:

- People generally don't leave reviews out of the goodness of their heart.

- Your competitors are likely incentivizing reviews. If you don't, there's a good chance you will fall behind.

- Decide how aggressive you want to be and how much risk you are comfortable assuming. I'm not saying to blatantly ignore Google, Facebook or Yelp's policies; I am just educating you as to the reality of the review building process for most local small businesses.

Create an Email List of Your Customers

I strongly recommend that you collect the email addresses of your past customers for the sake of review building. If you only have a handful of email addresses, you can easily contact them individually. Just a simple email will do:

Dear Susan,

Thank you so much for being a valued client. I just wanted to follow up with you to see if you would be willing to write us a quick review. If you would be so kind as to leave us a review, we will email you a $10 Starbucks gift card. Please email me back after leaving your review to claim your gift card.

Here is the link to leave your review:

(Link to the profile that you want to build reviews for)

The gift card is really key for a high conversion rate on these types of emails. You'd be surprised at how much a small offer can motivate a customer who would otherwise have zero interest.

If you have lots of email addresses on file (hundreds or thousands), then you will be able to build lots of reviews very quickly by using a product like ReviewShepherd (https:// reviewshepherd.com/). You can upload spreadsheets containing hundreds of email addresses into the software and create an email that is sent out to ask the customer for a review. It's like magic; the reviews come flying in.

There are many benefits to using ReviewShepherd for this:

- **Speed.** Rather than manually emailing customers, you can send out large blasts in just a few seconds.

- **Filtering of Negative Reviews.** Negative reviews are filtered out from being posted publicly online. If you have a spreadsheet full of 3000 customer email addresses, you might not know which customers had a great experience and which would bash you with a one-star review. ReviewShepherd directly emails you the negative reviews, rather than posting them online. Only the positive reviews go live.

- **Ease of Use.** ReviewShepherd makes the process of leaving a review intuitive and easy for a customer to follow.

If you don't have thousands of email addresses on file, but have lots of phone numbers instead, you might want to look into a service called Birdeye. They utilize text messages for the sake of review building.

Don't Go Overboard

I would recommend using a product as powerful as ReviewShepherd with a bit of caution. If you have four reviews total on Google that have been generated over the course of five years, it would look fishy to Google if suddenly you started getting ten new reviews a day. Be conservative, consider the policies and terms for each review site that you want to build reviews for, and use careful judgment regarding how aggressive you should be.

Insider Tip

Format your Google link in a way that directs the customer to the exact right spot to leave a review. If they're signed into a Gmail account, the box to select a star rating and leave a review will pop up for them. ReviewShepherd can help you with this if you don't know how. Here is an example of how your link should function:

https://www.youtube.com/watch?v=xB4Fro1kTz4

Yelp

I want to give Yelp its own section here because it's a different animal than other review websites. Tons of small business owners really hate Yelp, and I don't blame them. I personally hate working with Yelp; they have blatantly stolen from me. When I tried to call several times to make the situation right, no one was helpful or sympathetic, and no one made the situation right. They're almost as bad as working with a car rental or cable company! I have never understood why companies that generate billions of dollars of annual revenue would screw over and alienate a customer for life over something so trivial as $100, but many large companies make a habit of it.

They also really alienate small business owners with the following annoying practices:

- Their salespeople harass you constantly. No matter how many times you say that you have no interest in their advertising programs and to please remove you from their call list, they keep calling, keep harassing. By the way, for the vast majority of businesses, Yelp ads are a poor investment and the money is better spent elsewhere, like on Google Adwords.

- Yelp filters out a ton of reviews, many of which are completely legitimate. Think of the poor small business owner who had some bad luck with one customer and gets a one-star review (the business may have done nothing wrong but some people are just awful).

Upon searching for the company name in Google, searchers are greeted by the Yelp profile, which ranks second in the search results—right behind the company's website—and prominently displays the one-star rating in the search results. This kills the owner's conversion rate, so he pleads with a few of his customers to leave some reviews on the Yelp profile to get that star rating up a bit.

The customer spends a half hour leaving a really long, nice review and feels good for having done a good deed. Within hours, the review is filtered into the "other reviews that are not currently recommended" section. The owner and customer are both frustrated, having spent time and energy on an endeavor that has produced zero results.

- Let's say a couple nasty customers ruin your online reputation and you want to delete the profile because it's killing your business. Seems fair enough since you created your profile, added photos and optimized it—all of which helped bring Yelp even more traffic. You may have even spent a bunch of money on Yelp ads. Guess what? They won't allow it! https://www.yelp-support.com/article/Can-I-remove-my-business-page-from-Yelp?l=en_US

Alright, enough Yelp bashing. The truth is that they're a necessary evil for most small business owners because their website generates so much traffic and is a critical component of the online presence for most small businesses. For example, Yahoo and Bing pull Yelp reviews into their Maps profiles. Although I have focused almost entirely on Google in this book, it's a good idea to give Yahoo and Bing at least a little bit of consideration since there are at least a handful of searches that are conducted on their sites. ☺

If you're going to take a "glass half full" approach, consider the fact that if you really do nail your Yelp presence and have more five-star reviews than anyone else, it's possible that's the only marketing you will ever need. If, for example, you own a sushi restaurant in San Francisco and you have more five-star reviews on Yelp than anyone else in the sushi business, then you can pretty much forget about all of this complicated SEO stuff and any other kind of advertising efforts whatsoever. You're set.

My advice to small business owners: don't underestimate the importance of Yelp and make a concerted effort to maximize your exposure there with an attitude of patience and humility. Go into it knowing that you're going to get a lot of great reviews filtered out, be harassed by salespeople, possibly be stolen from, etc. Just embrace it and have persistence. Keep pushing to expand your presence on Yelp and try to have more good reviews than anyone else. In the long run, it will likely be worth it.

CHAPTER 8

Citation Building

A citation is a listing on another website that includes a reference to your company's name, address and phone number. Here's what it would look like:

Company Name: Bob's Company

Address: 123 Main Street, Suite 123

City, State, Zip Code

Phone: 123-456-7890

Citations are very important to local SEO. Google's goal is to serve accurate information to their customers, and citations reassure Google that the info they are serving up to users is correct.

If they are going to list a website in their search results, Google wants to make sure that the company is still in business, the phone number is correct, and the store location and hours are accurate. If a lot of incorrect information starts to populate Google's search results, then Google users will get frustrated and turn to other search engines like Bing and Yahoo. They could even go to—gasp!—the Yellow Pages.

All About Reassuring Google

Citation building is about communicating to Google, "You can trust that all of the information here is accurate, so you can feel comfortable sending one of your users our way."

You can leverage this by doing these things:

- Make sure your **company name, address, and phone number** are consistent. Also, try to make sure these things are always formatted in the same way.

  For example, if your company name is "Company Name Inc," you don't want it to be displayed as "Company Name" in some places and "Company Name Inc" in others. You also want to have the same phone number across all listings. I should note that some people make it sound like you need to be absolutely obsessive about name/address/phone number consistency, and that's not really necessary. If there are a few old listings out there with some inconsistent information that you're unable to get updated, it's highly unlikely this will cause any harm to your SEO presence.

- Include the citation (company name, address, phone number, website) in as many places as you can: alongside links you build, in social media profiles, in articles and descriptions of your company.

- Make sure that the contact information for your business appears all over your website. I have seen Google Maps listings that look fine, but the address listed is nowhere to be found on the company website.

A good way to get started with citation building is to sign up for one of the Moz Local packages: https://moz.com/products/local/pricing. Their product will create and update business profiles on a bunch of important directory websites, which leads to a number of quality citations for your business.

CHAPTER 9

Social Media

Social media definitely factors into Google's algorithm these days. Think back to the concept of Total Web Presence. Google is going to hold your website in higher esteem if you have tons of Facebook likes and Twitter followers, post frequently on Google+ (even though no one uses that stupid thing), have a strong following on Pinterest, and upload a bunch of YouTube videos.

Some people claim that social media (not Facebook Ads but the actual posts and interacting with people) can produce a high ROI and drive lots of sales. I think that's a hyperbole. I haven't observed it at least. The odds that a transmission repair shop posts something about differential service on Facebook and some random dude sees it and reacts by thinking, "Gee, whaddya know! My sis needs differential service I think I'll forward this to her!" are pretty low. You might randomly stumble across a lead in your social media efforts, but it's been rare in my experience.

From my perspective, social media for small local businesses only serves one purpose:

To help you rank higher in Google.

For this reason, I recommend you consider buying some Facebook Ads to generate some likes and comments, get a bunch of Twitter followers, and upload some videos to YouTube. Like blogging, if you don't have the time or don't want to bother with figuring it out, go to Upwork and hire someone to assist you. A word of caution: don't fall into the trap of trying to take shortcuts and buy a package of something like 500 instant likes on Facebook. Similar to bad link building practices, this method is unlikely to help and could even hurt. It's better to build slowly and organically.

YouTube Tips

You don't need to dump a huge amount of time and money into YouTube in order to obtain the SEO benefits. You could use your iPhone to record yourself answering some simple questions that would appeal to your target customers, for instance. There are lots of people who would rather watch a video to get the answer to a question than read an article about it.

If you don't want to create YouTube videos yourself, then find someone on Upwork to create them for you.

Include the videos on your actual website wherever it makes sense to. If you own a remodeling company and do a video about kitchen remodeling, then make sure to embed it on your kitchen landing page. This will help get your videos some views and likes. Time spent on website is a factor in Google's algorithm, so if you can keep someone on your website for an extended period of time while they watch your videos, that will certainly help your SEO.

You can buy cheap YouTube views directly through Adwords, for as cheap as a penny a view. It's a good idea to buy some views; it can only help your overall social presence in the eyes of Google.

Make sure to embed a clickable link back to your website in each video's description. Include your address and phone number too so that you get a citation out of it.

CHAPTER 10

Paid Search

Even though this book is mostly about SEO, I want to cover a few things about paid search here (not nearly enough – you could write an entire book about it). Everything works together with regard to your Total Web Presence. Traffic is a factor in Google's algorithm. If Google sees a lot of people visiting your website, clicking around to multiple pages, and spending some time there, it helps your SEO. Especially if you are launching a brand-new website, paid search (i.e. Google Adwords) is a great way to get the ball rolling.

Do everything you can to increase your click through rate and conversion rate. Do this by loading up all of the extensions that are relevant for you. Get a review extension with an A+ BBB rating popping. Make sure to sync your Maps listing to the account so that you can pop your office address/Google Maps star rating. Add in call extensions, sitelinks, etc. Read up about all of these things if you don't know what I am talking about; it's really important. (https://support.google.com/adwords/topic/3119075?hl=en&ref_topic=3119122,3181080,3126923,)

Don't Let Google Get the Best of You

Google is really great in a lot of ways. They have generally been helpful and good to me over the years; however, I do think they try to come up with lots of little sneaky schemes to maximize their revenue—many of which aren't beneficial to you, the advertiser. Always remember that Google didn't grow to be a $100 billion company by giving you free clicks through the organic search results; they don't make any money off that. Google might make money in some other ways now too, but people paying tons of money for clicks through Adwords has always been a gigantic source of revenue for them.

A few tips:

Location Settings

Under location settings, I would recommend the "People in your targeted location" option rather than the default "Reach people in, or who show interest in, your targeted locations." I never trust Google in these situations. I have seen them do too many crazy things to drive up the spend for keywords that will never convert.

For example, your flower shop that's located in Pittsburgh might miss out advertising to someone who lives in Pittsburgh but is traveling in Boston and types into Google "Pittsburgh florist," but you will avoid wasting money on people living in Boston who were just reading an article about the Pittsburgh Penguins and then typed "florist" into Google. This isn't much of an exaggeration; Google does crazy things like that sometimes.

Display Network

Make sure when creating your campaigns that you aren't opting into the display network; it's a huge waste of money with a ridiculously low conversion rate for most businesses.

Match Types

Use very little pure broad match. Set very low bids on any broad match and use those terms mostly as a keyword discovery tool. Over the years, I have had so many Google reps send over account recommendations, and the optimization tips include the addition of a bunch of pure broad terms with high bids. That would send the spend through the roof and conversion rate would suffer. No thanks, Google. Crawl through those search query reports regularly, add negative keywords to filter out anything that won't convert, and spend most of your money on *broad modified, phrase or exact match terms.*

Bidding

I don't like those enhanced bids and other bidding tools that Google offers either. I still prefer manual bidding. I have seen Google charge insanely high costs per click for terms that they claim are "more likely to lead to conversions," even though when I check out the search query reports, sometimes the term isn't even relevant. Best not to trust Google with things like that. They're a public company with an agenda to maximize profits.

Set Your Bid Wisely

In terms of setting the perfect bid, if you have perfect information, then the optimal bid takes two variables into consideration:

Conversion rate * Target cost per conversion = Optimal bid

Let's say you're trying to sell a hotel room and your PPC conversion rate is 2%. Your average profit per conversion is $300, and you decide that you're willing to spend up to $150 to acquire that conversion. In this case, your bid should be $3 (.02 * 150). You could actually bid a bit more than that because your actual cost per click always comes out to be lower than your bid.

The idea of having a budget when it comes to PPC can be a bit foolish sometimes. If there were some special machine out there in which you put one dollar in and get $5 back, then you wouldn't limit yourself to only putting $50 in. You would stick as many one dollar bills in as you possibly could.

However, that's not the reality when it comes to many campaigns; most clients want you to stick to a budget, which becomes a bit tricky. It would be really easy to find that optimal bid if conversion rate and position were completely independent, but that isn't the case. If your conversion rate stayed constant regardless of how high you showed up on the page, then it would be easy: you would just bid as low as you could to just barely hit the cap, and to get as many clicks as possible for the money. It's not that simple though. The higher you show up on the page, the higher your conversion rate is likely to be. There are two main reasons for this:

1. There will plenty of "lazy" consumers out there that will just go with the first good-looking option that they stumble across. They aren't going to search through ten different websites to find the very best option. I can fall into that category sometimes... the "lazy consumer."

2. All of the fancy extensions that help your conversion rate—such as location extensions, review extensions and call extensions—show up only if you're bidding to top positions. If you show up low on the page, you just get the most basic ad display.

Consider the complex interaction between these factors when determining your bidding strategy.

Landing Pages

Invest some time and effort into those landing pages. Have the phone number and contact form displayed prominently and consider implementing an online chat feature. Really sell the benefits of your company and explain why you're better than your competitors. Consider including some testimonials, and rave about your A+ BBB rating, your 400 five star reviews on Google, and things like that.

Optimize Your Ad Copy

Do the same thing with your ad copy. You want to convey that you are the best and build as much trust as possible. Write multiple ads and compare performance. Take both conversion rate and click through rate into consideration, and delete ads that aren't performing well.

Keyword Selection

Keyword selection can be really easy for many small local businesses. For example, if you're a DWI attorney in Cincinnati, you're probably going to be 99% covered with just eight total keywords:

+dwi +lawyer

+dwi +attorney

+dui +lawyer

+dui +attorney

+dwi +law +firm

+dui +law +firm

+cincinnati +dwi

+cincinnati +dui

There's no need to add hundreds and hundreds of keywords for most local companies.

If you want to see if there are any terms you might be missing, you can add the term "DWI lawyer" on pure broad match with a really low bid. For example, it may be that "DWI in Ohio" gets good search volume/converts well, and the broad match would likely find that term for you.

Learn more here:

https://searchenginewatch.com/2017/10/17/google-adwords-the-beginners-guide/

CHAPTER 11

How to Measure Your Progress

Here's a controversial statement for you: "Traffic should not be a primary goal or metric when it comes to local SEO."

Some would rage against a statement like that… but I know it to be true though. Traffic in itself accomplishes very little for most small businesses. Think of a small local roofing company that's located in Orlando for instance. They might crank out 1000 really awesome blog posts and pick up a ton of long-tail traffic from all over the world regarding all kinds of roofing-related queries about maintenance, waterproofing, restoration, etc.

Does that really generate revenue for their company? Probably not. What generates revenue? Someone who searches for "Orlando roofing company" in Google and sees the roofing company with 80 five-star reviews show up in the Maps section. The user *might not even click through to the website,* but just dial the phone number right into their cell then and there, resulting in a $20,000 job *that doesn't even register as a website visit in their Analytics software.*

For this reason, we don't even have a Google Analytics account set up for many of our local SEO clients.

It's all about efficiency, and time is money!

What to Measure

What should you measure then? And what tools should you use to measure them?

We use the rankings reports on Moz (moz.com) for every single SEO client. We use their reports to keep track of several things:

1. The rankings in the regular organic search results for our target keywords in Google, Yahoo and Bing.

2. Which keywords display a Maps listing as part of the search results, regardless of whether our client's Maps listing is currently popping for that keyword. This is a

helpful data point to keep track of. A client could call you saying that their call volume fell off a cliff, even though the Moz rankings report shows their keyword rankings in the regular organic results look fine. What if Google was displaying Maps results for 100 of your target keywords last week, but is only showing Maps results for 25 this week? There's your answer most likely. The structure of the search results changes frequently and that's not something an SEO company can control.

3. The percentage of terms that we rank for in Maps. Maps might display for 50 keywords, for example, and our client might show up for 40% of them.

It's also helpful to log directly into Google My Business and pull the impressions and clicks that the Maps listing is generating. That can be a really helpful metric for local SEO.

Call Volume and Sales

Call volume and sales are obviously the biggest metrics that are going to matter to an SEO client. Regardless of how pretty some other metrics might look (23% increase in traffic year over year!!!), if as their SEO client you don't get a lot more calls and sales primarily as the result of your SEO company's services, you should fire them.

Google Analytics can be a helpful tool for a lot of small businesses, but as I mentioned above, it's not completely necessary for all local SEO clients. It does, however, certainly help you to monitor traffic, which we'll discuss in the next chapter.

CHAPTER 12

Traffic

Let's say you have a really solid SEO foundation in place. You've nailed your onsite SEO, have some good links pointed at the site, a decent number of good reviews on multiple websites, have signed up for all of the relevant directories, and have a good number of citations. Yet your website still isn't ranking. What's the problem?

Traffic could be the culprit. Traffic is a very underrated component when it comes to SEO (in terms of attaining rankings). If no one is visiting your website, it's unlikely to rank high, even if you have nailed a lot of the other items on your SEO checklist.

You need to explore ways to increase your website traffic. Here are a few items that you can consider:

Online Job Postings

It's a core value of mine not to waste people's time… which is one reason why I hate all of the unsolicited sales calls and spam email that I receive. So I would encourage you not to utilize this technique if you aren't really intent on hiring anyone. People will be taking the time to write up cover letters and send in resumes and things like that.

If you are intent on hiring though, job postings online that link to your website on websites like Indeed and Craigslist are a great way to drive lots of traffic to your website.

Maximize the Distribution of Your Blog Posts

Wrote a particularly interesting blog post? Maybe your buddy who has about 8000 too many Facebook friends would be willing to do you a solid and post it to their Facebook page so that it shows up in all of their friends' feeds. That should generate some nice traffic for you.

Paid Search and Facebook Ads

Pretty self-explanatory. I wouldn't run anything just for the sake of gaining traffic, though; I would make sure that I have a positive ROI or at least break even.

Capture Email Addresses and Create a Newsletter

Think this one through before just jumping into it. Make sure you can really add value to peoples' lives before deciding to capture email addresses and send out a newsletter. I find myself unsubscribing from newsletters almost daily because I don't want the spam in my inbox and the newsletters offer no value to my life whatsoever (I have no idea how I end up on so many of these lists in the first place).

If you can really come up with something that's valuable for people, then this might be a good option for you—especially if you're able to build a solid subscriber base. Each email blast you send out will result in an instant blast of traffic to your website.

CHAPTER 13

What to Do If Your Website Gets Penalized

There are so many factors that weigh into how to best handle a penalization. There's not one blanket way to handle it. Some factors to consider include, but are not limited to:

- How much do you value your domain name? Is the domain name worth a lot of money? Do your customers have it memorized? Does it get a lot of direct traffic?

- How many really great links does your domain have pointed at it?

- How easy would it be to get those links updated to a new domain?

- How much time and money will you spend building and switching over to a new website, getting email switched over, and other transition-related difficulties? You might need to update the signage on all of your company vehicles, for example.

If you aren't absolutely married to your domain name and the transition wouldn't be too costly, then I would recommend starting from scratch with a new domain, website and content. You can update important profiles and directory listings (even the Google Maps listing) over to the new website and we haven't found any kind of carryover penalty. You can just take down the old site and implement a meta refresh that will direct people to the new site. I would stay away from a 301 redirect here.

If you are married to your domain name or don't want to transition for other reasons, then you're probably looking at a disavow report (https://support.google.com/webmasters/answer/2648487?hl=en) and link clean up. I don't like disavow reports, as I have not found that sites who have done a disavow ever rank as high as those with a completely clean reputation. I think Google views a disavow as an admission of guilt and that those sites have a kind of black mark on them indefinitely. If you're sticking to that domain name no matter what though, then you have little choice. Do the disavow and manually work (within reason) to get any bad links removed that are pointed at your website. I should quickly note that manually emailing webmasters about this—to request your link be removed—is usually a fruitless endeavor. It's highly likely that your link is one of thousands that shows up on the spammy website, and that they have received hundreds of emails regarding link removal over the years. The odds of them taking the time to get into their code and do you a favor by removing your link are extremely slim.

After executing your disavow/link removal, the SEO process is the same as that of any other website: it's just that excellent results are more difficult to come by. You might have to be more heavily reliant on paid search for your online leads in a situation like this.

CHAPTER 14

How to Hire a Good SEO Company

After reading this book, I hope that at the very least, you will have enough information to make a good decision about which SEO company you hire (assuming you don't want to tackle SEO yourself). Hopefully you have some tools to leverage in terms of asking some educated questions, as well as a better ability to distinguish truth from BS.

If going through the process of hiring an SEO company, I would go through the "How to Spot the Bad Guys" chapter one more time, and generally shoot for a company that does the opposite of all those things. A few other things to keep in mind:

- Ask for a rough price range of their services. If it's over-budget for you then don't waste their time and don't make any of the following requests...

- Ask to meet the actual account manager who you will be working with in the future. Sure, the salesperson might come across as super honest, intelligent and trustworthy... and that's exactly why they're in that position. Meet the people who will be doing the actual work for you and who you will be communicating with on an ongoing basis.

- Ask if they build links and how they build links. Ask them to show you five examples of links that they have built themselves in the past few months. Refer to the "Link Building" chapter in this book and screen the links to see if they meet the criteria for a good, safe, powerful link. Check the websites that the links are pointed at (their clients) and see where the websites rank.

- Ask how long it will likely take to get ranked. A really experienced expert won't be able to pin down anything precisely in terms of "we can accomplish exactly X by exactly Y date"; however, someone who is experienced and knowledgeable will certainly be able to say something like:

"You're in a good position when it comes to onsite optimization for your target keywords, backlinks and social media presence. The biggest problem that I see is that you're not popping in Google Maps as consistently as I would like, and when you do pop, one of your competitors has three times the number of five-star reviews. I'm sure they're getting a huge percentage of the calls. So we are mostly going to be working on some things to get that Maps listing to pop more frequently, and we are going to emphasize increasing your review count. I would think you will see an increase in rankings within the first month, and hopefully six months from now we will be in really great shape. I would think that your call volume will pick up greatly by then. If not, I would encourage you to fire us."

I can almost always nail a critical issue when it comes to this type of thing and give some idea as to what to expect when that issue is addressed. If the potential SEO company can't nail that, I would look elsewhere.

That being said, here's one final plea: please be respectful of people and treat them how you would want to be treated. Do you want people wasting your time? Didn't think so. If I had a dollar for every time that someone completely used me for free information (which is necessary to discuss before a contract is signed so that you're on the same page when it comes to a game plan – the process doesn't really work when an SEO company is super aloof) with no intention whatsoever of actually utilizing my services, I probably could have paid for a good portion of my new pair of completely awesome Armada Tracer skis with that money.

Conclusion

After returning home from the music festival and awesome motorcycle trip through the mountains, I found that my Australian Shepherd, who had an upset stomach at the time, had an accident all over the carpet. It was so disgusting. Talk about going from the highest of highs to the lowest of lows. So I had to drive over to the store and pick up some Nature's Miracle and clean it all up, even though it was late at night and I was tired. It was awful.

Oh well, focus on and remember the good things though. That will go down as one really awesome day...

... and if you don't take anything else away from this book, I hope that you will at least remember to *trust your skis*:

35098853R00058

Printed in Poland
by Amazon Fulfillment
Poland Sp. z o.o., Wrocław